TEAMS
ON
FIRE!

Transforming your group
into a more productive, profitable
and motivated team

*To Cindy —
I hope you enjoy this — Evy*

TEAMS
ON
FIRE!

Transforming your group
into a more productive, profitable
and motivated team

Heather Hansen O'Neill

Published by
RockStar Publishing House
28039 Smyth Drive
Suite 102
Valencia, CA 91355
www.rockstarpublishinghouse.com

Manufactured in the United States of America, or in the United Kingdom when distributed elsewhere.

O'Neill, Heather Hansen

Teams on Fire! Transforming your group into a more productive, profitable and motivated team

Worthy Shorts ID: RSP115
ISBN:
Paperback: 978-1-937506-41-4
eBook: 978-1-937506-42-1
PDF: 978-1-937506-43-8

Cover design by: Tayyaba Satti
Interior design: Darlene Swanson

Disclaimer:

The Author makes no representations or warranties with respect to the accuracy or completeness of the contents of this work. No warranty may be created or extended by sales or promotional materials. The advice and strategies contained herein may not be suitable for every situation. This work is sold with the understanding that the Author is not engaged in rendering legal, accounting or other professional services. If professional assistance is required, the services of a competent professional person should be sought. The Author shall not be liable for damages arising herefrom. Further, readers should be aware that internet websites listed in this work may have changed or disappeared between when this work was written and when it is read.

www.fireinfive.com

Contents

Teams on Fire! 1

Appreciation. 5

Body Power 9

Clarity. 13

Deliver 17

Empower 21

Ferocity 25

Grow 29

Happiness 33

Input 37

Justice 41

Keep it simple 45

Listen 49

Mentor 53

Noble 57

Ongoing communication 61

Plan and Prioritize 65

Quality 69

Responsibility 73

Structure 77

Time 81

United 85

Variety 89

Why 93

X-ray 97

You 101

Zig zag 105

Teams on Fire!

Transforming your group into a more productive, profitable and motivated team

"If your actions inspire others to dream more, learn more, do more and become more, you are a leader."

—John Quincy Adams, 6th U.S. President

Teams on Fire! guide

Who's the book for? This book includes concepts that anyone looking to improve his or her business relationships can use; however, it was written specifically with the Team Leader in mind, the person who spends a significant amount of time organizing, managing, directing and leading a team to success.

What you'll learn: There are already many wonderful books offering in-depth information on team building. But I realized there was a need for something different. I created a resource guide for inspiration and action that will reinforce the primary team-building concepts on a regular basis. Even if you have the inclination to read a 300-page book on the topic, you might not have the time. I wanted to make team building accessible for a busy team leader.

How to get the most out of it: Open this book to any page and you'll find a relationship-building idea you can implement to keep your teams positive, strong and productive. However, **Teams on Fire!** is best used if you read it from cover to cover first, then go back to the **Spark the Flame** section of each chapter to take action on one concept at a time. The way to get your teams fired up is to move from theory to practice as quickly as possible.

Why read _this_ book? Why use a book from an author who works with team leaders like you on a regular basis? Experience and success. I have helped many people learn how to build stronger business relationships with a special focus on team building. This includes work with sales teams, service teams, project management teams, executive boards and interdepartmental chaos.

Many times, if I'm on the scene, it means that the company or team is damaged in some capacity--people aren't getting along and are often working against each other, there's fear of project failure and miscommunication, and sometimes individuals' jobs are on the line. After serious work, they become more focused, productive, profitable teams, and ultimately the improved communication increases feelings of contentment and even joy for the people involved. My satisfaction comes from being a part of the transformation.

This book isn't meant to replace that process but to reinforce the techniques and empower the team leader with specific viewpoints and actions to ignite a more positive, focused, productive atmosphere. This is not a process- or system-intensive manual. My expertise is in relationships, and I believe that strengthening the relationship you have with YOU is what will light the way for those you lead.

Appreciation

"I would maintain that thanks are the highest form of thought, and that gratitude is happiness doubled by wonder."

—G.K. Chesterton, writer and philosopher

One of the leading causes of dissatisfaction in relationships is a perception of being underappreciated. Luckily it is one of the easiest and most cost-effective areas to focus on for improving communication.

In your sales and service interactions, or within teams, departments, levels or locations, take the time to find something you sincerely appreciate about each person. They will be more receptive, positive and willing to help you.

Within your team, find and support the traits and skills of the individual members. Understand that different people like different forms of appreciation. As you build deeper relationships, you will discover who prefers the quiet handshake and thank you, who enjoys a handwritten note, and who favors public recognition. It is the rare individual who would not like to be acknowledged in some capacity for a job well done.

Client Story: I was coaching a project manager at a struggling company. This company was cutting costs at every turn and had decided not to cover any more team expenses. When my client told me he had taken the team out for pizza and go-carting after their project ended, I asked him if the company had reversed its policy. "No," he said. "I paid out of my own pocket. The team worked hard and they deserved a little appreciation." This is why his teams were the most productive in the company.

You don't have to go out of pocket to express your appreciation, but as a team leader, the job of setting the stage for gratitude and approval falls upon you.

Customer appreciation and employee appreciation are the two primary areas of focus.

1. From a simple call on a birthday to special services, hand holding and constant communication, customer-appreciation efforts are effective ways to create customer loyalty and boost referrals.

2. Depending on the size or focus of the company, employee-appreciation programs can offer anything from thank-you notes all the way up to elaborate trips and gifts.

Employee morale is the overall outlook, satisfaction and confidence employees have in their workplace. The team leader's ability to find the skills and attributes to appreciate about their team members will help improve overall morale in the organization.

If you use this strategy of appreciation at home, it can have similarly astounding results. Relationship strategies can be used in many capacities and in all aspects of your life. The focus here is on business relationships and team building, but if you find something here that could improve your relationship with your children, spouse or friends, I'd certainly encourage you to apply it there as well.

But let's not forget that self-appreciation and gratitude can impact you internally, improving your attitude, focus and energy, and that can indirectly influence your team.

Personal Story: I was sipping a warm, sweet latte at Starbucks and pounding away on my keyboard next to 30 of my closest friends all doing the same, because most houses didn't have electricity and we didn't expect to get it back for at least another week. It was in the days after Hurricane Sandy, the third such storm in our area in just over a year. On my way to Starbucks, driving around downed power lines, passing houses with roofs caved in, and encountering an enormous tree across the road, I knew in my heart how very lucky we were. Hurricanes, earthquakes and tsunamis have been ravaging the world more frequently these last few years. What we experienced was just a big wind by comparison to many. We were very fortunate indeed.

Have you ever experienced a tragedy? Something that upset you greatly in the moment but which you realized later was exactly what you needed? Sometimes it takes years to see the benefit of a challenge. Wouldn't it be nice if we could experience all the value in the moment of the challenge? The ability to see an event for the significance and learning it offers *while it is occurring* is what differentiates the truly successful from everyone else.

Viewing any problem from another perspective, or from your future perspective, or with an eye to how it will benefit you or others in the long run can completely turn your attitude around. It can be the starting point of finding the solution.

As you navigate challenging team meetings, fret about productivity issues and worry that your project won't make the deadline, take the time to appreciate what *is* working, and find the lesson in the challenge. It will provide you with a more complete and useful picture as well as a more productive mindset.

Questions to Ponder: What are you grateful for in this moment? What's working? Is there someone who needs appreciation for his or her hard work or contribution? How can you turn around a challenge and use your insight and wisdom to find a new solution?

Spark the Flame: List 10 things you appreciate about your job, your life, your team as a whole, and each person on the team.

Body Power

"Good for the body is the work of the body,
good for the soul the work of the soul, and
good for either the work of the other."

— Henry David Thoreau, author

Your most intimate and enduring relationship is the one you have with your body. It can be used in many different ways to alter your state and, believe it or not, improve your business relationships.

Your ability to understand others at a deeper level and create more powerful relationships will improve when you become aware of the messages your teammates are sending through their body language. Becoming more attuned to the intricacies of your teammates' communication will make you a more informed leader.

In addition, being aware of your body language can help you better align your message and communication style. You will become more authentic, believable and credible with your awareness of these concepts.

Client Story: After giving a keynote speech recently, I saw a woman leaning against the nearby table with her arms crossed, obviously waiting to speak with me. Many people had rushed over to ask me questions about my team-building presentation or ask me to sign their book. I got the feeling that this woman was angry with me for the delay. But when it was her turn, she told me how much she'd enjoyed my content and energy, and that she was thinking of hiring me to coach her. Her manager had told her that the other people on her team couldn't relate to her and "felt a relationship disconnect that was creating animosity." She didn't understand why and wanted to change this perception. I suspected, and later confirmed, that her body language was incongruent with her thoughts and feelings. She didn't realize how much her body had been putting up a barrier in building relationships. It almost cost her her job.

What message are you projecting? You're a leader, but is your confidence noticeable in your posture and eye contact? Are your arms crossed or open and inviting during team discussions? Is your smile genuine? Do you stand to begin your meetings to take control of the agenda and then sit to mirror the team when you are requesting feedback? Simple awareness about the power of your body to communicate can help you make minor adjustments that will increase the team's view of your competence, strength and rapport.

You can use this same awareness to better understand others. Watch the facial expressions, gestures and body placement of your team members. Try it at your next meeting: If you see fidgeting, a lack of eye contact, and other distracting gestures, it's time to do or say something more engaging. And if you see pursed lips or a furrowed brow, you might want to pull the person aside later and ask if they have any questions or concerns.

Personal Story: Recently I was watching a movie with my boys, and after an exchange between the two main characters, my 11-year-old turned to me and said, "Mom, she likes him." This was interesting, because at this early point in the movie the characters hadn't expressed their real feelings, and the girl had just told the boy to leave her alone. So I asked my son, "Why do you think so?" And he said, "She told him she didn't like him, but look at the way she's looking at him and how she's holding her hands. She looks like she really does like him."

My son is already learning a valuable life skill: the ability to pick up on all the clues that others are communicating. Among words, tone and body language, it's body language that sends the most clues.

Interesting note: We've heard a lot about the power of the mind over the body, with scientific research showing the benefits of laughter therapy and positive thinking on healing. But it's not as commonly acknowledged that this is a *reciprocal* relationship. When you're feeling stressed, dejected or low-energy, moving your body can alter the state of your mind. This is one reason exercise is so important. Even a brief break from the computer to stand, stretch, or walk can reenergize, lift your spirits, and infuse you with new creativity and productivity. Use this to your benefit before meetings or to release stress any time of the day.

Questions to Ponder: Are you comfortable using body language to communicate? Are you good at picking up on other people's signals? What can you do to improve? What activities can you add to your day to create more energy and focus?

Spark the Flame: At your next meeting, be aware of the message you are sending with your body language. Then determine two changes you want to make to construct a message more congruent with your intent.

Clarity

"It is one of the commonest of mistakes to consider that the limit of our power of perception is also the limit of all there is to perceive."

—C.W. Leadbeater, theosophical author

The ability to set clear expectations for your team is an essential management skill. Ambiguity causes stress. You don't want a team of stressed-out people. It's a ticking bomb of miscommunication and petty quarrels ready to detonate.

Have you ever been in a situation where you were unclear as to what your boss, spouse or friend expected of you? You may have felt confused, anxious, frustrated or angry. Asking for clarity when you don't fully understand instructions shows initiative and will contribute to your success.

When it comes to achieving personal and professional goals, measurable specificity is required. Whether you are setting examples, receiving instructions, or establishing guidelines and goals, clarity and perspective are key.

Client Story: I was facilitating a management meeting for a financial services company. There was some frustration because two dominant members of the meeting were arguing, and others in the room were uncomfortable. Nothing was getting accomplished. As I was getting ready to break it up and offer a suggestion, I noticed an interesting facial response from the woman who was refilling the coffee station. As a student of people, I quietly went over to her and inquired. She had listened to the argument without bias, and she hesitantly whispered in my ear a simple, yet brilliant, compromise. When I asked her to share it with the group, she looked at me like I was crazy, but then she complied. They loved her idea, and the CEO later invited her into a management role in the company.

Personal story: I am like a sponge. I ask questions, extract suggestions, research what's working, and brainstorm options with many different people. I process what I learn, accept recommendations that fit, and at times I'm spurred to action based on my strong emotional opposition to what has been offered. I get the most fired up when someone tells me I can't do something because it hasn't been done before, it won't work, it's challenging, or there's not enough time and resources. Challenge motivates me. However, I doubt I would be as effective if I went around proving people wrong without also accepting help when I need it.

What about you?

Have you ever felt like you were walking through a hot, dense jungle of life? You can't see two feet in front of you, you get pricked by thistles and thorns, and the sounds around you make your heart pound in fear.

Everyone experiences challenge and strife at times. When we're in the thick of it, our inability to see what's around the bend, as well as the constant poking and nudging of negativity, can be frightening. What do you do when this happens to you?

Do you freeze in terror, become immobilized?

Do you run scared, pushing and slamming your way through, with no sense of where you're going, feeling mildly better with movement and action...even if it's taking you in circles?

How about climbing a tree?

Imagine how different the jungle would appear from up high. You could be amused by the swinging monkeys, taking in the raw beauty of the landscape, realizing that awful sound was simply the mating call of a beautiful bird, able to see exactly where you need to go.

You'd have a new perspective. Perspective provides clarity.

Are you too close to a situation? Overcome by confusion, challenge and fear? Try to find a new perspective. Look at what's happening from a different viewpoint. Imagine what it would look like in 10 years. Investigate all the options. How might an expert navigate it? Ask questions.

The ability we have to look at our lives from various perspectives affords us the insight to continually grow and become more than we ever thought possible. Wisdom is knowing what we don't know. Courage is asking for help to find it. Success is the compilation of the two.

Questions to Ponder: Can you make the expectations you set for others clearer so their comfort level is higher? Is there something you are currently uncertain about that needs clarification? Who can you ask? Is a new perspective in order? How can your team benefit from an increased, conscious focus on clarity and perspective?

Spark the Flame: Incorporate a discussion about expectations into your next team meeting. Ask for feedback as to whether expectations need to be clarified and whether the communication in general needs to be more transparent. Accept comments without judgment; later you can go back and review them and choose the best suggestions and options for improvement.

Deliver

"You are what you do, not what you say you'll do."

—Carl Jung, founder of analytical psychology

When you buy scissors, you expect they will cut. When you turn on your windshield wipers, you anticipate they will clear your windshield. When you purchase milk and pour the first glass, the expectation is fresh, cold, delicious milk. And when you send a letter, you presume it will be received.

In business, and in life, when someone tells you they will deliver something, you trust that you will in fact receive what was promised. It takes only one disappointment to destroy that trust--and many promises kept to win it back.

Delivering goes hand in hand with setting clear expectations. Your team needs to set the expectation of what and when you can deliver and then follow through on the promise. Your effectiveness will be judged on your ability to promise and deliver consistently, over and over again.

Opportunities abound to create loyal clients who become your best source of new business when you to go the next level and exceed their expectations.

Client Story: I was working with a spa services company on a minor internal riff between the partners. Thankfully, the communication gap within the company wasn't apparent to its clients. In fact, they did a superb job of exceeding their customers' expectations. The spa offered manicures, pedicures, massages, facials and many rejuvenating treatments. In addition to high-quality treatments, the spa delivered many seamless services. One in particular stood out to me. Though manicures were probably the business's lowest-profit service, even clients coming in just for manicures would also receive a chair massage, a heated seat, and a deliverable that truly exceeded expectations: the manicurist would walk out with the client, start her car, and buckle her in so she wouldn't ruin her new nails. Obviously, this was a very busy salon. This thorough understanding of how to help the customer maximize the service is what overdelivering is all about.

If you are a project manager, you're dealing with numerous people who are involved in delivering the team objective. The assignment requires understanding what the shareholder and sponsor expect, what your team can deliver, what the end user receives, and any discrepancies within this complex model. Discrepancies create a state of stress for you, the team leader. Strong communication with updates and minor adjustments are essential to your team's success.

Personal Story: I had several big projects and clients around the time I was writing this book. The deadline came upon me as if from out of the blue, when in fact I should have known. Time was tight, and many people said I couldn't do it. Other authors told me stories of extending their deadlines. People with "good intentions" offered their insights on why it was unreasonable to think I could deliver on my promise. I'm not sure where it came from, but I have always felt strongly that if you misjudge a deadline, overpromise or underestimate your skills or resources, it's on your shoulders to get creative and try every solution before surrendering to a missed deliverable. Obviously, if you are reading this book, it means I uncovered a solution, sleep deprivation notwithstanding.

When you deliver on your promises, people make assumptions about your ability to do it again and again. And when you don't, the same applies. Customers talk. What are people saying about your company? Your team? You?

> Reliable • cutting-edge • poor • outstanding
> mediocre • dependable • inferior
> inconsistent • satisfactory • exceptional

Questions to Ponder: Do you deliver what you promise in your sales and marketing? What do you do to exceed your clients' expectations? Is there anything else you could do to ensure a more consistent delivery of products and services?

Spark the Flame: Make a list of all the times you have exceeded your customers' expectations. Is there anything on the list that isn't yet, but could become, a consistent application for your team or company? Make a conscious effort to include it in your deliverable system.

Empower

"Don't confuse poor decision-making with destiny.
Own your mistakes. It's OK; we all make them.
Learn from them so they can empower you!"

—Dr. Steve Maraboli, speaker and author

Provide the tools for your team to do their jobs well, and then set them free to do it.

"It takes too much time to teach someone else to do it. I'll just do it myself."

"I'm the only one around here who gets anything done!"

"If you want something done right, you have to do it yourself."

Have you ever said things like this or heard such comments from others in your organization? If so, stop right now and take a hard look at your team productivity. Empowerment is a way of doing business that may take time to set up, but ultimately it's far more effective for reaching goals with a loyal, happy team.

Client Story: A point-of-purchase display company hired me to evaluate its customer service department and develop training to promote superior service. One primary issue was blocking the way to better service: a system that took away the power of the front line, which created apathy, blame and frustration. According to company policy, when a customer called with a problem, there was nothing the customer service team could do to solve the problem. But once the company empowered the front-line people with specific guidelines (for example, for complaints under $100, they had the power to refund the customer), they were more confident, friendly and service oriented. The client walked away with a quicker resolution, making repeat business more likely.

The more you live in the world of short-term, emergency-driven, reaction-oriented approaches, the more likely you'll be forced to stay there. If you don't take the time to work on your team or business, you will remain on the hamster wheel of stress and catch-up.

Personal Story: I was working as a sales and service manager when I came up with the concept for my business. While golfing with one of my clients, I hesitantly told him my idea. I was taken aback by how positive and encouraging he was. He told me he wanted to be my first client. If I failed, he would tell no one, but if I succeeded, he would tell everyone. How empowering! Making the leap to entrepreneurship was frightening, but knowing there was someone who believed in me was extremely motivating.

Why is it important to cultivate an empowered team?

People tend to live up to your expectations of them. When there's a positive environment of continual support and trust, you can ask employees to get a project in on time and they'll bend over backwards to make it happen. If you've taken away their power, if they feel like you don't respect their opinions, or if they're afraid a mistake will result in major repercussions, then negativity and blame will be the team culture.

Quick Team Leader Reminders:

1. Take the time to teach. Train your team on the system, the required skillset and especially the decision-making process.

2. Provide positive encouragement for those who take responsibility and make the effort.

3. Don't offer your opinion on how you would do things differently unless it's absolutely necessary. There are more ways than one to get to a solution.

4. Remember to give credit where it's due, when someone does something right.

It may take more effort to foster an empowered setting, but you won't regret it. In the long run, the team will be happier and more productive. People want to feel like they are contributing.

Are you a team member who would love more responsibility, trust and respect? Ask for more ownership of your work. Tell your team leader that you are committed to contributing, and request any additional tools you might need to increase your skills.

Questions to Ponder: Do you currently work or lead a team in an empowering atmosphere? If not, can you see the value these strategies would bring to the team? What can you do today to foster more empowerment within your team and at your company as a whole? Any other ideas come to mind?

Spark the Flame: Choose one person you feel deserves, and would be receptive to, more responsibility. Schedule any necessary training. If you feel a need to micro-manage, make a conscious effort to give the employee a specific amount of time to try the task on his own. Look for ways you can encourage and praise.

Ferocity

"Life's up and downs provide windows of opportunity to determine your values and goals. Think of using all obstacles as stepping stones to build the life you want."

—Marsha Sinatar, educator and author

When you are fired up about a project, your energy and excitement can be contagious. Teams have been known to overcome insurmountable odds through the power of an inspired leader. Think of the leaders you've known who stand out as having a mission, a message and a capacity to find the good in a challenging situation. Think about the people who have changed the world. They were ferocious.

Ferocious: intense, strong, unstoppable, determined, competitive, extreme, fierce.

The feeling of ferocity is visceral. Ferocity is when an idea of the mind deeply impacts the body. It manifests as an inability to remain immobile, energy, confidence, and a conviction to achieve greatness.

Your team may be experiencing difficulty, but if you're able to embrace solutions you inspire confidence and encourage productivity and respect. There are many different styles of ferocity. You can be dynamic and upbeat to fire up your team, but you can energize them just as well with a quiet strength and by setting a strong example.

Client Story: I was working with a nonprofit fundraising team that wasn't performing up to par. Some on the team had been fundraising for years and some were rookies. There was a distinct lack of energy and creativity. We had brainstormed options, but there was no fire. The woman who had started the nonprofit was present, and I asked her to tell her story of why she'd started it. As she spoke of her personal tragedy, her desire to make a difference, and her goals for the organization, there was a beautiful light in her eyes and a quality in her voice that was quite touching. Everyone was impacted. Leaning forward, listening intently, a few even wiped away tears. They were getting Fired Up. Her strength and ferocious protection of all that she was striving for was evident and awe-inspiring.

Don't be afraid to share your story.

Personal Story: Not long ago, I was chatting with a friend when a great idea struck me. I popped up to go check something. He leaned back in his chair, shook his head, and put up his hands as if in surrender. "What?" I asked. "I'm not getting in your way," he said. "I've seen that ferocious look before." He's been a friend for some time, and apparently I have a "tell"-- I get this weird look on my face when I'm determined. When this look appears, those closest to me know to back up and wait it out.

Discomfort can also create a ferocious response.

Have you ever said something that you desperately wanted to take back?

Or tripped in public, and turned and looked at what you tripped over with disdain, as if it had been the object's fault?

Have you ever gotten to a point in business where you wanted to give up because it was just too hard?

Have you ever been uncomfortable?

Discomfort. What is it? Where does it come from? And how can we use it?

Discomfort is defined as "mental or bodily distress," "something that disturbs or deprives of ease." It's that feeling inside us that creates a pain in the pit of our stomach, makes us shake in fear or spurs our feet to run away.

We feel discomfort when things are no longer easy. And when challenge arises, it can be tempting to run away, give up, just to stop the pain.

But nothing spectacular comes without some challenge. A diamond becomes a diamond after experiencing high temperatures and extreme pressure. People truly appreciate the greatness that comes from effort. It makes the reward taste that much sweeter.

Think back to a time in your life when you felt you quit too early, when you felt that if you had stuck with something just a little longer, through the hard part, you might have been able to realize the opportunity fully. Do you ever experience regret?

My challenge to you is to put yourself out there and embrace discomfort. Begin to enjoy the shaking and the pain in the pit of your stomach. Because you know that if you work through it, just a little longer, you will be rewarded. Make that conviction. Most people don't. Most people give up. But do you want to be "most people"? Or do you want **MORE**? Get ferocious.

"The truth is that our finest moments are most likely to occur when we are feeling deeply uncomfortable, unhappy or unfulfilled. For it is only in such moments, propelled by our discomfort, that we are likely to step out of our ruts and start searching for different ways or truer answers."

—M. Scott Peck, psychiatrist and author

Questions to Ponder: Is your team on fire? Are YOU? Do you have a story you can tell to inspire? What else can you do to create a focused energy for your team? What provokes that ferocious determination within you? How can you harness it?

Spark the Flame: What thought/idea/solution is so powerful that it generates a visceral reaction within you? How can you replicate that for your team? Hold a special brainstorming meeting for outrageous, cutting-edge ideas. Watch the body language of the team. When they lean forward, talk faster, and get "that look" in their eyes, you should seriously consider implementing whatever precipitated it.

Grow

"When we are no longer able to change a situation,
we are challenged to change ourselves."

—Victor Frankl, Holocaust survivor and author

The most successful people are continually improving themselves, reading, learning and growing. When you believe you know everything there is to know about your industry, your company and your clients, you are on a dangerous path.

Continuing-education classes, business books, online workshops, research, discussions with someone farther along on the business or life path...there are countless ways to grow.

How can this help your team? It will set an example. Your continual improvement and learning will garner their respect. Encourage everyone to develop their skills and contribute to the success of the team.

Client Story: A cutting-edge manufacturing company brought me in to implement a DiSC assessment. (DiSC is a behavior-assessment tool based on the theories of psychologist William Marston and excellent for use in training and development.)

I was to facilitate a discussion on how to use the tool to communicate more effectively. This company was applying an original idea to encourage growth and development: Each week a different manager would be the "Idea Master," charged with taking five minutes of the meeting to recommend a book, a new idea, or a resource to try. One week the Idea Master suggested my program, and that's how I was introduced to the company. The number of stimulating concepts they came up with in those five minutes per week was astounding.

What do you do in business when you need to learn something new to get to the next level?

> Read a book?
>
> Search online?
>
> Ask a mentor?
>
> Take a seminar or class?
>
> **Train.**

What do you do to get your body in shape or ready for a performance of some kind?

> Stretch to prepare the muscles?
>
> Create a plan and keep adding more intense workouts?
>
> Ask for help from someone who has done what you want to accomplish?
>
> **Train.**

So what do you think you need to do to overcome any blocks your team is experiencing or to create a more cohesive, productive group?

TRAIN.

If you want to get to a new level in your business and your life, you need to step outside your comfort zone and train your body and your brain for something bigger, more powerful, more impactful...**MORE.**

You cannot continue to do the same things you've been doing and expect the MORE to miraculously appear. You won't be ready for it. For some, it means training your mind to believe you deserve more. For others, it means training your body to bring you into a positive state of mind when you are being "fed" negativity. For yet others, it means creating a new pattern of extreme actions that are more likely to bring the changes you crave.

If you want a stronger team, you need to change things up. Learn something new. Model the team success of others or adopt an idea and make it work in your world.

Questions to Ponder: What new ideas can you pursue for your development? Does the team require additional training? Can you implement a new routine in meetings where different team members can offer new resources? What other ways can you support growth?

Spark the Flame: Introduce the "Idea Master" strategy to your team.

Happiness

*"We tend to forget that happiness doesn't come as
a result of getting something we don't have, but rather
of recognizing and appreciating what we do have."*

—Frederick Keonig, inventor

Have you looked at the faces of the people you pass on the street? Most are stressed, angry or distracted. There is a frightening increase in dissatisfaction all around us.

How would you describe the energy at your company and within your team? Is there gossip and backstabbing or have you developed a fun, positive, happy and well-adjusted group?

Work doesn't have to be as boring and painful as the word would imply. As a matter of fact, happier employees are more productive and more likely to go the extra mile for their leaders. Teams spend a lot of time focusing on goals and end results. As you might have guessed, I'm a proponent of such proactive attention. But it's equally important to their overall satisfaction that they enjoy the journey in getting to the goal.

Thrive on challenge, celebrate small accomplishments along the way, and lead with grace.

Client Story: I met a lovely woman at a distribution company where I had done some interpersonal-relationship training for the information technology department. She was a beacon of light, always smiling and giving of herself. She would bake brownies and leave them by the coffee area, put together the company team to walk for the American Cancer Society, and always be the first to offer to pitch in and help when needed. She was one of those unique individuals for whom happiness and serving are part of their chemical makeup. Some people find this type of person highly irritating simply because the concept of perpetual happiness is foreign to them. But the owners of this company had a different view: They realized what a prize she was and wanted to express their gratitude, letting other employees know they valued helpfulness and positivity. At one of the big company meetings, they surprised her with an award and gave her the official title of Happiness Guru. I heard there wasn't a dry eye in the house.

Personal Story: I've found my happiness in the balance of peace and mayhem. I can teach yoga on a beach in the morning and fly on a trapeze in the afternoon. I can immerse myself in writing or speak to a group of 4,000. I can love my children more than life itself and still be grateful when they leave for school. For me, happiness is found in the variety of life's experiences. Many who struggle have never taken the opportunity to discover what happiness means to them.

Uncover the commonalities of what brings joy to you and what brings joy to your team, and you will be able to incorporate approaches and team habits that bring smiles and constructive energy.

Whether you want to garner a bit of motivation for a final push to achieve your goals this year, or you seek constant inspiration to guide you, or you want to be a conduit for spreading enthusiasm to those around you, here are a few tips for you:

1. **Review**- Look at what has gone on in the past one to six months. Acknowledge the successes. See the challenges for what they really are; don't give them more power than they deserve. Find the lessons.

2. **Track**- Make note of what's working and keep doing it. Discard any old processes that aren't serving you well. This applies to people, too--limit the amount of time you spend with highly negative ones.

3. **Revive**- Look at the goals you set for yourself. Are they still valid? Do they need to be tweaked? Anything need to be added? How can you get excited about them all over again? Do the same for your team objectives.

4. **Assess**- What needs to happen for you to get where you want to go? Lay out all the steps that need to take place. Prioritize what is most important on a daily, weekly and monthly basis.

5. **Activate**- Take action! Find someone to whom you can be accountable. Tell them what you plan to do. Then do it. Accountability stimulates action.

Understand that your future lies in your hands. Your choices determine what you achieve and how much you enjoy the process along the way. Life is a series of selections that create a beautiful mosaic that nourishes and supports the unfolding of who we were always meant to be. The choices you make for your team, where you focus your energy, and the systems will define the consistency, productivity and happiness of the members.

Questions to Ponder: Are you happy? Do you want to be? Is there a way you can take happiness more seriously? Look at your team from an outsider's perspective and ask if someone who doesn't know the group would consider it a happy, productive team? How can you create a more positive mindset? What one action can you take today to make someone on your team smile? Can you celebrate the accomplishments of the group and the members more?

Spark the Flame: Incorporate one new team habit that makes people smile. You can get your crew involved by holding a contest or putting one person in charge of team happiness per month.

Input

"For me, just being on the cover of a magazine wasn't enough. I began to think, what value is doing something in which you have no creative input?"

—Elle Macpherson, actress, model, businesswoman

Feedback is crucial to growth. You might not like what you hear, but most feedback has value. Knowing how you are being perceived can lead to small adaptations that lead to greater achievement. Notice I said small adaptations. A minor tweak in the way you're working can have tremendous impact.

Ask for input from the team on how you're doing as well as on processes and systems, and solicit their suggestions for project facility. Ask for input from sponsors, shareholders, customers--everyone who is impacted by your team's success. Customer and employee surveys are powerful tools used by the most successful companies and teams.

Client Story: I am a designated speaker for an international CEO group. The benefit of this group is that the members not only learn from the speakers, but the ensemble takes on the role of a board for each CEO. They present their challenges and ideas and the group members offer input based on their individual experience and expertise. Everyone benefits greatly from the collaboration. I also run an entrepreneurial mastermind that runs on the same premise. The members take turns on the "hot seat," and the rest of the group contributes insights.

Have you ever been involved in a mastermind group? Napoleon Hill, author of *Think and Grow Rich*, first defined the mastermind as a "coordination of knowledge and effort, in a spirit of harmony, between two or more people, for the attainment of a definite purpose." When you give your time, your wisdom, your honesty, your respect, and your creative juices to help others in the group succeed, they in turn challenge you to achieve your own amazing results. An innovative team can be created and run the same way.

Personal Story: I've found a direct correlation between inclusive parenting and better behavior. Greater camaraderie and cooperation come from children who are asked for their input on important family decisions. Whether in regular family meetings or in decisions on family rules, consequences, and where to go on vacation, their input in the process makes them feel respected and important.

Regarding your team, ask for input *regularly* so that they are used to the process and prepared to respond, rather than taken off-guard.

If you're going to ask for ideas from the team, you need to be willing and able to act on them. Obviously not all input is actionable, but if you invite suggestions and receive a good idea, then you must be willing to use it; otherwise future requests will be met with silence or cynicism.

Questions to Ponder: Do you ask for input consistently enough? Are there additional people you should be including in your requests for feedback? Are you able to implement the ideas? How can the process be more effective?

Spark the Flame: Right now, list the top five team challenges that require a decision or action. Choose one to bring to the team for input.

Justice

"All the great things are simple and many can be expressed in a single word: freedom, justice, honor, duty, mercy, hope."

—Winston Churchill,
former Prime Minister of the United Kingdom

People need to feel, with conviction, that their leader is fair. Do you take different viewpoints into consideration and make objective decisions? Do you consider the individual in your assessment, with the understanding that fair may not always mean equal?

Build a strong relationship through open-minded, decent and reasonable interactions. When you have built trust with your words, your honor, your actions, your consistency, people will stand behind you.

The less emotionally attached you are to a situation, the more likely you'll be able to offer a reasonable assessment. That moment just prior to your response is critical. Resist the impulse to immediately say or do something in favor of taking a moment to breathe and process. This technique will serve you well and reduce your need to apologize for impulsive behavior.

Client Story: When I am invited to present a keynote for a large company meeting, I send a questionnaire and offer to talk to several people within the company to gather stories and lessons that would customize my speech. During this process with an insurance company, it struck me that everyone had praised a particular key executive. When I asked why, they all responded with some variation of "He's the fairest person I've ever had the pleasure of working for!" During the keynote I used this story to make a point. Afterward he came up to thank me. He never realized how much his way of doing business impacted the employees. They notice and appreciate it.

Personal Story: I sat down with my son's second-grade teacher for a conference. My son is a spirited boy, and most of these conferences involve discussions about reining him in. This teacher, however, greeted me with a smile and said, "Your son is such an interesting boy. I enjoy having him in my class. He keeps me on my toes." I love a teacher who's up for a challenge, so we had a great discussion and she told me a story. One day the class was discussing parables, and my son shouted out (something most teachers don't appreciate), "Oh, it's like karma!" Even though he was right, the teacher didn't think he really knew what it meant. She asked him to clarify. He said, "When I do something wrong, like push my brother, sometimes it comes back to me in some other way...like tripping down the stairs. That's karma." Although it wasn't an all-encompassing explanation, he understood the concept of ethical consequences.

There are consequences to our actions, and the capacity to take responsibility for our actions can be powerful. Setting an example and encouraging that in others is part of true leadership. Do you believe that if there were no consequences, there would be no reason for doing something? Or is doing the right thing the right thing, whether or not anyone knows you did it?

Have you ever heard the Rolling Stones song "You Can't Always Get What You Want"? It was never one of my favorites until I really thought about the lyrics: "If you try sometimes, you just might find you get what you need." Certain challenges and opportunities come your way because they will teach you a lesson or because they hold something perfect for you that you didn't even know existed. That is a beautiful form of justice.

Questions to Ponder: Do you consider yourself a just team leader? Would others agree? Is there anything you can do to increase consistent, rational consequences? Are your choices serving your team? And are they serving you?

Spark the Flame: Begin a practice of taking a breath when you feel an emotional reaction to a situation. Give yourself time to respond appropriately.

Keep it simple

*"You must learn a new way to think before
you can master a new way to be."*

—Marianne Williamson, author

Have you ever overcomplicated your work, your relationships, or your life?

In the world of team building, I see this over and over again. We become attached to complex processes, hold on to grudges, and continue with outdated, convoluted chains of communication.

Simplify.

Client Story: I did a keynote speech for an athletic group's awards banquet. The gentleman who recommended me was a coach. He invited me to one of his basketball games to meet some of the players a few weeks before the banquet. I came early and watched the warmup. I don't know a lot about basketball, but I understood everything he was saying. "Shoot the ball," "elbow in," "move your feet," "use the backboard." That all seemed pretty basic to me, but his team was number one in the league. I asked him about it afterward and he said that no matter how good you are, you can never go wrong by practicing and perfecting the basics.

Does your team need to get back to basics? Is training in order? Or do you need to simplify your processes? And what about you, personally: Do you need to simplify your life and rejuvenate?

Personal Story: I have been known (picture me sheepishly scuffing my foot in the gravel) to keep going and going and doing and fixing and running...until my body gives out, or some very nice person sits me down and sticks a glass of wine in my hand.

I recognize my challenges, and I've been striving to change these tendencies. I've actually gone outside my comfort zone and asked for help. I have shut down and watched a silly movie. I've taken a week-long vacation with no computer and checked messages only once a day. And guess what? The world kept turning. People kept breathing. And life went on as if this colossal lack of productivity didn't matter.

And here's the massive epiphany: I was more productive after taking the necessary downtime.

The body, mind and spirit need to renew and rejuvenate in order to effectively function. Just as we need sleep and sustenance to restore our physical bodies, we also need peace and joy to replenish our souls.

When you work too hard, you can get run down and lose your ability to effectively manage your responsibilities. Recharging your batteries makes you more creative, more industrious and probably, truth be told, more fun to be around.

*"As long as a person is capable of self-renewal,
they are a living being."*

—Henri Frederic Amiel, philosopher and poet

Both personally and professionally, keeping it simple can serve you greatly with increased productivity, focus, energy and a positive mindset.

Questions to Ponder: Are you stressed and in need of downtime? How can you rejuvenate? Is your team working on systems that are too complicated? Are there basic standards or practices that need to be learned or reinforced? What else can you do to simplify?

Spark the Flame: Take a close look at the flow of communication, the way you use technology, and your overall team process with an eye on how to simplify and increase effectiveness. Make necessary changes.

Listen

*"Too often we underestimate the power of a touch,
a smile, a kind word, a listening ear, an honest
compliment, or the smallest act of caring, all of which
have the potential to turn a life around."*

—Leo Buscaglia, author

Shhhhhh.... Can you hear that? That silence is a golden nugget of opportunity.

Building strong relationships is best accomplished by taking time to listen. Often we are filled with ideas and opinions and want to share them with our teammates and coworkers. But if you stop and listen first to what the other person has to say, you're far more likely to walk away enlightened and appreciated.

Collaborative teamwork begins with respect. I believe so strongly in it that I would go so far as to say it's an obligation to listen intently. At times your teammates and clients don't even realize what they need or want until you've allowed them to talk it through. You do them a great service by listening with an open heart.

Client Story: I recently ran a full-day success workshop with a focus on relationship building for entrepreneurs. In addition to my presentation, the guest speakers, and the panel of experts, there were also breakout sessions on specific areas of interest, which I facilitated. The Business Development Group was lively and great ideas were flowing. But I noticed that certain members of the group were speaking more than others. We had already discussed different behavioral styles using DiSC, so everyone understood that lingo. I said, "Ok, I see our D's are dominating the conversation," which met with laughter because D's are the dominant, leader-style people. "Let's make sure that for each discussion point we let the C's and S's answer first, alright?" They understood that the C and S styles were more reserved and wouldn't jump in with their ideas. But when asked, they offered many great suggestions. The takeaway points for everyone in that breakout session were outstanding.

Whether you are familiar with the DiSC behavioral assessment approach or not, I'm sure you know there are people on your team who naturally offer their ideas, take over in leadership roles, and dictate the direction of the conversation. You need these leaders and can use their unique skills to initiate action, but powerful teams nurture a range of competencies and styles. The ability to elicit interaction from the more reserved members and listen to everyone on the team in turn will go a long way toward building rapport and developing insight.

Personal Story: A family tradition we've established that you can use with an excitable team is to assign numbers. My three pre-teen boys would invariably ask me questions or share their ideas simultaneously. It was stress-inducing, until one day when I said, "OK...1, 2, 3. That's the order--Go!" And they calmly took turns telling their stories, and I intently focused on them each individually. The point is to give everyone a turn and listen closely. Your focus and respect will be appreciated.

Questions to Ponder: On a scale of 1 to10, where would you rate your listening skills? Do you like it when people look you in the eye and sincerely focus when you are speaking? Is there a way your team meetings can promote better listening? Where else in your life would this skill serve you?

Spark the Flame: Listening is a skill you can acquire or perfect with practice. Commit to being completely in the moment for at least one conversation each day. Make eye contact, listen carefully. It won't be long before it becomes a much appreciated habit.

Mentor

"Significance comes from helping others."

—Lou Holtz, football coach

"She needed a positive role model."

"I saw the way he looked up to me and it made me want to be better."

"I became a mentor to help someone in need. Little did I know *I'd* be the one who would forever be changed for the better."

When speaking at a mentoring conference, I received these comments among the replies when I asked, "Why do you mentor?"

The benefits of insight and accountability for the mentee are obvious, but I've found that the mentor benefits just as much. It's a beautiful, symbiotic relationship.

Client Story: One service I offer in my business is executive coaching. In that role, I spend much of my time in a mentoring capacity. But I firmly believe that the more you know, the more you know you don't know, and it pushes you to continually strive to learn something new every day. Of course I have my own coaches who have mentored me along my path. My most recent coach met with me for what was supposed to be a quick drink and a chat. Three hours later, I left with a sheet full of ideas on how to streamline a new aspect of my business and tools for assessing its financial viability that I hadn't considered. That conversation proved very worthwhile.

Personal Story: I recall the wonderful stories and lessons my grandparents used to tell me. My parents live far away, and I longed for my children to have the same positive experience I remembered. I inquired of the men and women at our local senior center and found that many were missing grandchildren who lived far away. So I connected the seniors with a group of local families to bring together the two generations to spend a little time knitting, playing chess and, most importantly, sharing stories. The program was well received by all.

Internal company mentoring provides less-experienced employees with support, skills, and insight and wisdom from others who are farther along on the career path. A strong bond forms as the relationship deepens. Benefits for the mentee include training unlike any other, having a sounding board for ideas, and making faster progress on the path to success. Benefits to the mentor include enhanced leadership skills, reflection on best practices, and the satisfaction of giving back.

As a team leader, you have the chance to be a mentor to a member or members of your team. I recommend you take the opportunity, create an open-door policy, and give of yourself fully.

You likely have a trove of stories to share and nuggets you've learned through the years. Sharing these gifts will make your team stronger as a whole.

In addition, seek out someone higher in the organization that you respect and admire for qualities and skills you hope to achieve. It might be frightening to ask that person to mentor you, but more often than not, people are honored to be asked. Barring serious time constraints, he or she may take you up on the request.

Questions to Ponder: Have you ever had a mentor? What was the biggest benefit you received? Have you ever mentored someone? Do you see the value there as well? What is the advantage to your team if you incorporate more mentoring of and among the members? How can you implement this new policy if it's not already in place?

Spark the Flame: If you don't already have a mentor, begin with that relationship. Make a list of the people with whom you'd like to connect. Reach out and request a meeting to start the mentoring process.

Noble

"The principle of worthy intent is the inherent promise you make to keep the other person's best interests at the core of your business relationship."

—Ed Wallace, radio personality

This concept of noble intent includes a focus on character, honesty, integrity and values. It's a concept we'd like to see more of in our society.

When we focus on doing the right thing, on being our best, on serving, there is a positive energy that permeates the group. A cyclical element of mutual cooperation occurs. This provides us with a guideline for right actions that benefits everyone.

Many businesses focus solely on profit, without concern for community repercussions. Some focus on giving and fail because they didn't keep an eye on profits. Your team and your company can be viable and still contribute to the betterment of your community and society as a whole. A good balance is necessary. Do the right thing, for the right mission, and be fairly compensated for it.

Client Story: I love working with companies that understand their responsibility to the community. A beverage-company client of mine impressed me with its desire to leave a positive legacy. The owners believed in the interdependence of business and the world. They spent time researching and implementing green building alternatives. They initiated a program to contribute to worthwhile charities that meant something to their employees. Of course, they were one of the first on board with my community-giveback program, **Stop the Violence, Embrace the Children**. This type of wisdom and compassion does not go unnoticed. More and more customers have been seeking out businesses with a sense of community connection and contribution.

> *"There is no better exercise for your heart*
> *than reaching down and lifting someone up."*
>
> —Bernard Meltzer, Radio host

It's simple, really: See the big picture of the world and your part in it. Then do what you say you're going to do, whether anyone is watching or not.

Personal Story: There are times when we aren't honest with those closest to us. There are times when we're not honest with ourselves. We often present ourselves in different ways in different situations or inadvertently act in a way we "should" as opposed to authentically. As a speaker, I joined a speaking organization. I learned many things. In addition to basic techniques such as reducing filler words, using body language, and using vocal variety, I learned a style that was approved of in the industry. It worked for many people.

I controlled my wild style, chose my words carefully, and staged my movements. My speeches were becoming very good. But one day I went to a presentation workshop outside this group. The facilitator was very open and direct. After my first flawless (or at least I thought it was) presentation, he said, "Who the heck was that?! I wanna see the girl I met at check-in who was energized and a little crazy. I'd pay to see her. This speech was boring. I wouldn't pay to see that!"

Of course I was upset. I had worked hard on presenting my material effectively. But later, his words hit home: I wasn't being me. I wasn't being authentic.

Now I balance technique with authenticity. I embrace my exuberance while still presenting a professional, clear message. Be authentic. Be you. Honesty, authenticity, and being true to your beliefs and values are all part of integrity.

Are all your team players permitted to be who they are at their core? Are there guidelines on how to act in situations that arise regularly? Is honesty cherished?

When something happens in a company that is sketchy or confusing, hiding only confirms guilt. Confront with confidence any challenge you face. Always be yourself. You are the only person you have to live with every day of your life.

Questions to ponder: Are you true to You? Is there a policy of integrity and character in your company? How are you fostering authenticity? Is there a cause the team can work on together to better serve the community and build a stronger bond?

Spark the Passion: Ask your team for suggestions of a project you can work on together that will promote goodwill and unity. Take a vote or put the suggestions in a bowl and pick one each month.

Ongoing communication

"Much unhappiness has come into the world because of bewilderment and things left unsaid."

—Fyodor Dostoyevsky, novelist

Sales: Collecting cards at events as a way of networking for new business and strategic alliances doesn't work if you don't follow up.

Service: Customers who aren't informed when there's a delay or change to their order can become irate. Irate customers might not tell you they're irate, but they'll tell all their friends and family not to use you.

Project Success: Sponsors that aren't kept abreast of changes in scope or deliverables of a project will become frustrated.

Teamwork: Team members who don't communicate on a regular basis may be wasting time duplicating efforts.

And if you, the team leader, aren't aware of things falling through the cracks soon enough to remedy the problems, you'll end up going over budget, missing deadlines and jeopardizing your next promotion.

Ongoing communication is vital in all areas of business.

Client Story: A small printing company where I was doing training was in a state of panic when I arrived one Monday morning. Apparently they had accidentally botched a job worth $300,000 for a large, high-profile client. If this small company had to eat that mistake, there could be grave consequences. I was met with "This is serious...what do we do?" comments. I looked at them and simply said, "You already know." They knew they had to tell the client while they could still make amends. Of course, they had already anticipated my response, which is why they were in a panic. However, being proactive (combined with their superior communication with, and results for, this client in the past) led to a conversation and compromise that rectified the problem without putting the printing company out of business.

Personal Story: As a communication and relationship expert, I understand the importance of ongoing communication. I try to apply it at home by being a resource, support and source my boys can turn to no matter what the situation is. But you have to know your audience. You cannot sit active boys down and say, "It's time to talk"; it doesn't work. Action is a better way to precipitate conversation. If you spend one-on-one time throwing the ball or hiking, they are more likely to open up and share their fears, hopes and concerns. Doing this regularly will build a strong relationship and open the communication lines for tougher conversations.

Know how your audience likes to communicate. Some people prefer a quick email. Some like a call. Others appreciate in-person connections such as lunch and coffee meetings. Using a wide variety of communication tools will help you find the right fit. Asking for the type and amount of connection your teammates and other important players prefer will take the communication to the next level.

Delegating is necessary to free your time to manage and lead the team effectively. However, even when you delegate, you're still responsible for the outcome, which makes ongoing communication even more imperative. Follow-up with team members about the progress and outcome is crucial.

Benefits of ongoing communication:

1. All parties are on the same page regarding expectations, process, timelines and problems as they arise.

2. Potential challenges can be seen and addressed before they expand to the point of no return.

3. Improvements can be identified, better systems can be implemented, and feedback can lead to new, more proactive procedures.

4. Stress is reduced.

If you are an entrepreneur and your team is your company, recognize that one-time clients don't transition into loyal, long-term proponents of your business if you don't communicate regularly. Communication with your team, your vendors and your clients should never cease. Don't get complacent once you have the client or once you think your team is on board with your mission.

Questions to ponder: What are you doing right in the arena of communication? Where are you lagging? Are there best practices of where and when to communicate? How can you improve? What might be blocking ongoing communication success?

Spark the Flame: Look at your overall communication with your team. Choose one way you can improve in consistency or quality of follow-up. Implement it by the next team meeting.

Plan and Prioritize

"A journey of a thousand miles begins with a single step."

—Lao-Tzu, philosopher

Creating a plan for the steps that will lead to your desired outcome is part of the "map" that we'll discuss later. Organizing a plan and prioritizing the steps helps action flow more easily. As a team leader, you are well aware of the importance of planning and prioritization.

People tend to be good at either planning or action. It's not often you find a leader who's superbly adept at both. But both are important. You already understand the importance of planning and prioritizing, and you practice both every day, but it couldn't hurt to learn additional strategies for elements that are so critical to the success of your team.

Client Story: I work a lot with project management teams, and I see a clear pattern. One of the biggest issues is that the people from different areas who are brought together for a specific project also carry with them the priorities, agendas and time constraints of their regular position. It's very difficult for a project manager to motivate an ad hoc team to concentrate on the project objectives and deadlines--difficult, but not impossible, if you can get everyone on the same page. Inspire a connection to the project mission. Be compassionate about the members being pulled in different directions. And work together to plan and prioritize the best solutions.

Depending upon the applications of your team, your project may have specific timeframes and expectations already assigned. If your team is your company or a division or department, then determining objectives and action steps is an ongoing process. Choose one primary target to focus on at this moment.

What are the tools required to achieve the desired outcome of this project or goal? Give the team the tools they need to do the job. Would you expect a baseball team to use a basketball? Would you fail to provide military personnel with proper weapons? Would a chef feel comfortable with no spoons or measuring cups? What are the ingredients for your team's success? They include a positive environment, open lines of communication, proper information and resources, and review. Make sure your team has the resources and information they need to get the job done.

Prioritize the steps to reach your destination. This may be one of those "I know this already, Heather!" moments, but you'd be amazed how many of my clients struggle because they haven't properly prioritized. The most important step should come first; yet many push that aside when there is a perceived emergency (someone else making a ruckus loud enough to distract you). Take steps starting with the most important and in the logical order in which the actions need to occur, and you will pave the way to success.

Devise a way to keep track of team progress, and then give everyone a deadline to work toward. Adjust as necessary and take additional action. Choose and do. Repeat. I'm simplifying on purpose here because most people overcomplicate action. Don't allow fear, procrastination, perfection or confusion to keep you from taking the essential steps toward a successful project or objective conclusion. The goal is to make sure the plan is good for the team and the organization as a whole.

Personal Story: I am an entrepreneur, and planning and action are both vital to the realization of my goal to have a viable business that contributes to the world. Action is my forte; I've never failed for lack of trying. I need to concentrate more on planning, the area needing the most improvement. My mentors and coaches in the industry help me lay out the precise process and steps required to achieve my ambitious goals. Then my strong will takes over to make it happen. One of my goals is to have a certain number of books, CDs and other products to support my clients in reinforcing the relationship strategies I teach. For that to happen, I must decide on the timeframe for the products and then backtrack the process to determine what steps to do in what order. To create a book, I need to understand how much time is needed for publishing, layout, editing, cover design and marketing. Only then can I know how much time is needed for writing, word-count parameters, and deadlines for submission. The writing flows and the goal of a book like *Teams on Fire!* is realized when planning and action converge.

Confidence plays a key role in achieving your team and personal goals.

1. Have you ever regretted holding back and not asking for what you wanted?

2. Have you ever wanted to express your concerns or ideas, but *fear* got in the way?

3. Ever felt like you left money on the table by not asking for a sale?

4. Is there something you want to have, do or be, but you haven't been able to make the jump?

If you answered yes to any or all of these questions, consider for a moment the power of confidence in overcoming fear and taking action. Look at the most successful people you know. Have they confidently asked for what they wanted? Have they taken chances?

Of course, everyone feels unsure at times. But the happiest, most successful people confidently move forward anyway.

Questions to Ponder: What is lacking in the area of planning for your team? Is there something you can do to incorporate more time for planning? If you already have a plan, have you put your goals in a format that includes immediate priorities? What are your weekly priorities and how can you make time for action? Can you do something this week to step outside your comfort zone and build more confidence?

Spark the Flame: Choose your number-one priority for the week. Put it into your calendar or delegate it. Then tell someone to ask you if you achieved your goal by the end of the week. Accountability spurs action.

Quality

"Do your best every day, and your life will gradually expand into satisfying fullness."

—Alexander Graham Bell, inventor

Today's world is in a "fast-paced, express line, get it done yesterday" time warp. People are simultaneously shaving, texting and driving. No one reads the second part of a letter or email if the first part doesn't grab their attention. It's all about the "hook."

I admit it. I am a product of this environment. I'm rarely able to turn off my phone without at least a slight worry that I'll miss something.

But I have to ask: How is this serving us? Are we building businesses, legacies, relationships that last? Or are we simply repeatedly satiating an ever-more-frantic desire for immediate gratification?

It takes time and effort to create an effective team. Quality is key.

Client Story: This story has to do with the quality of leadership. My worst memory from the beginning of my training career involved a client in the healthcare industry. I should have turned down the project. During the sales call, my intuition told me the business owner wasn't respectful and would be a challenging client, to say the least. Because I was just starting out, I took the client and tried to quiet the voice of concern in the back of my mind. I was brought in to train the customer service team to be more effective at providing superior service. The owner's introduction of me sounded something like this: "You guys are awful. Our clients are complaining and things have to change. I spent a lot of money to bring Heather in to knock you guys around and show you a thing or two. If you don't listen and change your ways, you're outta here!" He smiled at me and brought me to the front of the room. I was in shock. As you can imagine, the customer service team glared at me with animosity seeping from their pores. It was horrible.

There's no substitute for quality. Quality leadership inspires a team to action. Quality service ensures long-term customers. Products must be of good quality to endure in the marketplace. Evaluate progress in each area, adapt and adjust as necessary.

Many industries and products have specific quality-assurance programs which demonstrate to their customers that they have certain guidelines and standards of excellence. Some customers will do business only with companies that have invested in these programs.

In industries where there aren't as many regulated standards, it becomes more of a differentiating factor to exceed clients' expectations via superior service and quality products. What part does your team play in promoting quality control?

Personal Story: I recently saw an impressive picture of Gallarus Oratory on Dingle Peninsula, County Kerry, Ireland. Gallarus Oratory is an early Christian church thought to have been built sometime between the sixth and ninth centuries. Constructed with stones from the region, slightly angled, and <u>no mortar</u>, this structure has stood and endured the elements for centuries. Why?

Was it the faith, dedication and skill of the craftsman? Was it the devotion to the ultimate purpose of the building? Was it the time taken to carefully select and perfectly fit the stones together? Or was it the innate wisdom that things of value are worthy of time and commitment?

What are you building?

Do you want to have a business that is substantial enough to sustain you and your family and give back to the community and the world? Are you willing to devote the proper time to the building blocks of success: communication, cooperation, creativity and competence?

Do you want to be recognized for leading a team that goes the extra mile to attain a high level of productivity and profitability? Are you the type of leader who's respected for his/her focus on quality relationships, products and services?

With skill, time and dedication, you can build a team that, like Gallarus Oratory, will weather any storm. And remember that the tools, like the stones that were indigenous to Ireland, may not be far from reach. Have conviction in the value of your goal and open your mind to the help that surrounds you.

Questions to Ponder: When no one is watching, do you still do the same actions to produce quality products and services? Look at the quality of your team effort. How would you rate it? What are you building? Is there anything else you should be doing?

Spark the Passion: If you don't already have a quality-assurance process in place, research the best options for your industry. Make a proposal including timeline and purpose to the powers that be.

Responsibility

"One of the first things successful people realize is the old adage, "If it is to be, it is up to me." This doesn't mean that you do it all alone. It simply means that you take responsibility for your life and your career."

—Jim Rohn, author and motivational speaker

Personal responsibility appears to be severely lacking in the world these days. Passing the buck or blaming others doesn't serve anyone—and why give up one of the few powers within your control? You have control over what you think, how you feel, and what actions you take...and not a lot else.

I urge you to cultivate an atmosphere of responsibility on your team. Praise those who consistently demonstrate responsible behavior. When there's a mistake, let them come up with solutions for fixing it. Things will happen; it's how you react that determines character and success.

Client Story: One of my clients in the textile industry had locations in New York, Illinois and South Carolina. When a client would call the New York office about a delivery delay, they'd respond with something like, "I'm sure it was the office down South...they are so slow!" When a disgruntled client would call South Carolina, a representative from that office would say something like, "Did those fast-talking New Yorkers pull one over on you? I'm so sorry!" And they both labeled Illinois as "not knowing what they are doing over there!" We brought them together to facilitate discussions and work toward a shared vision. They realized how similar they were and even came to appreciate and like each other. This led to working together toward the common goal of pleasing the client. And overall customer satisfaction soared.

Personal Story: My 10-year-old son taught me another life lesson. We'd had a tough morning, and I had to take away one of his privileges to help him learn to make better choices. He was NOT happy, and he spoke harshly to me.

But in the car about 40 minutes later, he said, "Mom, I think I get it. The reason I get mad and blame you is really because it's harder to blame me. I need to start taking responsibility for what I've done."

Picture Mom joyously dancing and singing internally while responding calmly, "Wow, that's a really important lesson that a lot of adults don't always get. You should be very proud of yourself."

And it's true.

Anytime we struggle, it's usually because we have a lesson to learn. But as soon as we learn the lesson, forgive ourselves and others, and take responsibility for our choices and emotions, we are able to fully live this moment and release anything that might be keeping us from moving forward.

What do you have left to learn?

Questions to Ponder: Are you taking responsibility for all you should? What are your team practices regarding blame and responsibility? Is there something you can do to generate a consistently cohesive and accountable environment? What can you do today?

Spark the Flame: Institute a "pass the buck" fine. Every time someone makes an excuse before figuring out their role in the situation, they have to pay a dollar. At the end of the month or project, use the money to celebrate. Want to make a bigger impression or have a bigger celebration? Make the fine substantially higher.

Structure

"The important thing is not to stop questioning. Curiosity has its own reason for existing. One cannot help but be in awe when he contemplates the mysteries of eternity, of life, of the marvelous structure of reality."

—Albert Einstein, theoretical physicist

As you've most likely already discovered, having a structure in place to guide your team exponentially increases your chances for success. It ensures a better flow for productivity and consistency in replication, and it maps out the route so that everyone is headed in the right direction.

Many companies that have specific project management offices already use a set methodology and standards. Tested processes ensure consistency from project to project.

Any company that wants to have a consistent philosophy guiding all its operations but has yet to create even a manual will benefit tremendously by increasing organization and procedures.

Client Story: The owners of a small, rapidly growing manufacturing company had been hands-on for too long. The company was bursting at the seams. The owners tried to continue their policy of overseeing everything, but sales were good, time was short, and things were falling through the cracks. I came on to consult with them and found that my relationship expertise wasn't really what they needed. I recommended another consultant who specializes in creating procedures and manuals. This way the process that had been working for them on a small scale could be duplicated for the larger model, with modifications to ensure their success and continued growth.

Systems such as these guide you in reaching the goal of a stronger, more profitable business and more successful team members.

Personal Story: I recently gave in and purchased a GPS system for my car. I'm certain I was officially the last person with a car to buy one. But I have an excellent sense of direction, so I never thought I needed it. Until I started getting clients in obscure locations with no street signs. I got lost six times in two weeks. It was time.

When you are in unfamiliar territory (working with a new team?)...

and you are following directions (that are unclear because they stem from different agendas?)... ,

the chances for error, confusion and not meeting the goal (missing deadline, going over budget) increase significantly.

Ineffective or inconsistent practices result in miscommunication, mistakes, frustration and repercussions that could gravely impact your team and/or your job.

Questions to Ponder: What are your current best practices? Do you need additional systems to get everyone on the same page and moving in the same direction? Where should you begin? Is there someone who can help you?

Spark the Flame: Create a framework for making decisions and resolving conflict. What types of decisions are autonomous and which should require a chain of command? What steps do you want the team to take when a disagreement occurs?

Time

"Time is more valuable than money. You can get more money, but you cannot get more time."

—Jim Rohn, author and motivational speaker

Make an investment of time in your relationships. It will pay dividends. Teams that use their time wisely are less stressed, more productive and more profitable by far.

One of the biggest issues I work on with teams is reducing miscommunication. It's a huge time waster that directly impacts your bottom line. If you waste three hours a week, at $100 dollars an hour, on a six-month project...you've wasted $7,800. We all know that $100 an hour is very conservative and three hours a week wasted on miscommunication is exceptionally low. We also know that when there's a time waster, it doesn't affect just one person in a bubble; multiple people and projects are impacted, multiplying the cost to the bottom line. The time and energy I spend helping teams prevent miscommunication produces exponential cost savings and profit increase.

Client Story: I did a discovery appraisal for an insurance company. Their weekly meeting was lengthy and inefficient, they duplicated many processes, and they weren't using the strengths of the team members to their best advantage. Redistributing tasks, tightening up the meeting agenda, and developing a simple system for daily work with the client saved them a minimum of 30 hours a week. How much more profitable do you think this made them?

So if time is your most precious resource, how and where are you wasting it? How much does that cost you?

"I don't have time!"

"I'm just too tired after a long day's work."

"There aren't enough hours in the day."

"Where does the time go?"

"Dost thou love life? Then do not squander time, for that is the stuff life is made of."

OK, that last one was Ben Franklin. But have you ever found yourself saying something similar to those other quotes? I know I have. And I've definitely heard them a few too many times from clients and friends. For some reason, the biggest excuses always have to do with time.

But we all have the same amount of time. Some of us make better use of it than others. Why are some people wildly successful in accomplishing their goals while others are continually behind? Time management has a lot to do with it.

The term "time management" mildly irritates me. It's overused and rarely understood. To save a few moments of your precious time, I won't go into all the details or definitions of time management. I'll just say it's "the ability to use the time you have to accomplish your most important things."

Let's break that down:

"The ability to use the time you have" = Understand that we all have 24 hours, that's 1,440 minutes, or 86,400 seconds, in a day. What are you doing with your hours? Are you making the right kind of impact on the world with your time?

"...to accomplish your most important things." = Time often gets away from us. We get called upon to do things that are important to others but don't contribute to our goals. We get asked to do more than ever before. And everything is labeled "Urgent!" The first step is understanding the problem. Are you working toward your objectives?

The most successful people know what's important and DO IT FIRST.

Personal Story: When I ask myself why my closest friends are my closest friends, I realize the answer is typically because they have made an investment of time in the relationship. Time is a very valuable resource. If you ask yourself who in your circle has offered it to you in a significant, almost unconditional way, the list narrows down considerably. But the appreciation I feel for those friends is immense, along with my willingness to do all in my power to help them when they need it.

"To me every hour of the light and dark is a miracle, Every cubic inch of space is a miracle."

—Walt Whitman, poet

Questions to Ponder: What is most important to you? What is most important to the members of your team? What are the blocks to achieving that goal? Are there any current time wasters? What can you change to use your time more wisely? Ask for suggestions from your team.

Spark the Flame: Begin the process of valuing time--both yours and your team members'—by setting and keeping to a specific meeting agenda. If longer side discussions break out, you can schedule a separate meeting for those involved. Do not waste everyone's time by digressing on matters that do not pertain to the agenda. This will be greatly appreciated by the productivity-conscious people in the group.

United

"No one can whistle a symphony.
It takes a whole orchestra to play it."

—H.E. Luccock, minister and professor

Years ago I heard the expression "You are only as strong as your weakest member" from a friend in the military. That certainly applies in battle, but I believe it relates to business teams as well.

A team is a cohesive unit in which each individual's actions affect the group. It's like riding a bicycle with a flat tire, or synchronized swimming with one member who can't swim, or a high-performance team with no shared mission, vision or values. It just doesn't work.

Is there a common bond that holds your team together?

Client Story: This example involves a family-owned restaurant. As a relationship expert, I've found that the complex family/business dynamic creates challenges, at a minimum, and frequently leads to painful discontent. When I was brought in, this family was at a point of such frustration that they were considering dissolving or selling the business. The father had started the business, the eldest daughter was the COO, and the son was in charge of marketing and client relations. The main issue was between the father and the daughter. They had similar styles, both leaders with a clear idea of what they wanted and where they wanted to go. The problem was that the father thought the daughter's ideas were too risky and the daughter felt the father's were old-fashioned. The son suffered in a continual state of mediation, which was impacting his job and his health. As an outside source facilitating their discussion, I helped them understand that they were in agreement on the vision for the business: Everyone wanted a family-friendly restaurant offering quality food and a comfortable place for the community to gather. Compromise was the only way to achieve that goal. The daughter realized that her father's consistent, yet conservative, ways had made the restaurant into the popular gathering place the community currently loved. The father recognized that his daughter's ideas were innovative and could help them grow into something he hadn't even thought possible. The son breathed a sigh of relief.

Unlike in a family business where all the team members are intimately aware of one another's strengths and flaws, the challenge with most teams is in turning a group of very different people, from different backgrounds and experiences, with different ideas and goals, into a cohesive entity that uses those differences to make the sum greater than its parts.

What are the primary factors in creating a unified team that connects and performs?

Each team member should have specific expertise and credibility and be an innovative thinker. Each should consider himself a significant piece of the puzzle. A spirit of collaboration, where the team is receptive to give-and-take and shared resources, is helpful. Effectiveness improves when members are held accountable for their particular roles and responsibilities.

Know who's on your team, what motivates them, what excites them, what special talents and skills they bring, and appreciate them for who they are and how they contribute.

In our quest to achieve more in life, self-appreciation and humor are valuable tools. Look within and assess your strengths, challenges and ways of adapting to what life throws your way. Instead of judging harshly, as many are prone to do, try instead to view any faults with humor.

Personal Story: I'm not the most patient person on earth, but as I strive to improve through yoga, meditation, and counting to ...1,000, I also try to find ways to laugh about it.

According to the studies of Dr. Lee Berk and Dr. Stanley Tan of Loma Linda University, laughter can lower blood pressure, reduce stress hormones, and increase the level of infection-fighting T-cells. It truly is the best medicine.

No matter what you're seeking--to make more money, to be a better team leader, to grow your business, to become a better person--take the time to appreciate who you are and what you have, and find the humor in each situation. Think for a moment of the person in your life who makes you laugh the most. Make sure to spend more time with him or her. And if you can't think of anyone, go find someone.

Questions to Ponder: Do you consider your team a strong one? What makes it strong? Are there areas where you can foster more bonding and rapport between the members? Can you do a better job of making sure that everyone is in alignment with the mission of the company and each specific project? Where can you infuse a little lightness or humor?

Spark the Flame: Think of one action you can do to bring the team together as a collective, cohesive unit, such as a team-building activity like a ropes course, or a fun evening outside the work environment. Put it on the calendar for sometime within the next three months and talk about it to build excitement.

Variety

*"I saw the angel in the marble and
carved until I set him free."*

—Michelangelo, artist

We are all angels in the marble, each beautiful in our own unique way.

Appreciate the individual differences of the people who come together on a team. So often we judge and focus on dissimilarity, where we could instead be thankful for the power of diversity.

Successful team leaders search out differences; they identify each person's unique gifts and cultivate them. One might have strength as an inspired leader. Another might be highly organized and great at follow-through. Yet another might be persistent at finding solutions. And don't forget the relationship-focused people who tie us all together.

It's true that these differences will mean the team members have diverse concerns and ways of communicating that could potentially create conflict. But the more you teach the team to appreciate the benefits and strengths of each individual, the less conflict you'll experience.

Client Story: I enjoy facilitating executive brainstorming sessions because high-level executives are already aware of their strengths and the power of the creative process. These sessions are effective because the facilitator can encourage the participants to focus and contribute without being judged, which elicits a flow of ideas and solutions. One such session produced an idea for a new division of the company that resulted in the highest profit margins and growth the company had ever experienced.

Personal Story: When my company started growing and I needed to hire an assistant, I interviewed several people and ended up choosing a sweet young woman who was vivacious and ready to take on the world. Oh, and she was petite and blonde too, like me. I might as well have hired a clone. Of course it didn't work out, because her strengths were my strengths, so no one filled in the gaps where we were both weak. After I became a DiSC facilitator, which gave me a greater understanding of different styles and the importance of diversity, my hiring process improved greatly. My rapport with the interviewee became a smaller part of the process, and I shifted my focus to finding talents and skills that I was lacking. It made my future employees, and the company as a whole, flourish.

The DiSC self-assessment behavioral tool can help team members make the most of their individual strengths while adapting for improved communication and productivity.

Creativity is one way business teams can enhance variety and innovation. In business, creativity is often what distinguishes the companies that flourish from the ones that flounder. The ability to look at alternative solutions and adapt can set you apart and ensure a thriving business, even in the toughest of economic times.

Can you open your mind to using, instead of wasting, more of the resources you already have? How can you adapt what you are doing to better serve your clients or differentiate your company from your competition?

"Mind mapping" produces more creative solutions than you might expect. The process involves a diagram that uses words, thoughts and tasks around key concepts to help you brainstorm additional ideas or options. There are computer applications for it, but I prefer the feel of paper for stimulating subconscious solutions. Creativity may come naturally to some, but it is also a learned behavior. You can practice and improve your ability to brainstorm flexible options, and thereby improve your business and your life.

You can practice creativity by changing your perspective and seeing things in a different way. Try it today: During one interaction, put on the other person's viewpoint as if it were a coat. You don't need to agree with it. Simply see and feel it. You can take the coat off, or discard it completely, or try a new one. The simple act of trying on will have altered you in a positive way. Other ideas include navigating your house with the lights off. Go slowly; toe stubbing isn't supposed to be part of the process. You can also take a new route when traveling to or from work, or taste a new food. Try something new every day.

The same thing applies in your personal life. How can you create a more flexible work schedule to give yourself more time to play? What activities can you add to your lifestyle that will simultaneously energize you, increase your fun quotient, and help you be healthier?

Questions to Ponder: How can you embrace the variety that already exists on your team or in your company? Is there a way to foster more of it? Do you have any ways to enhance creativity? Can you think of other options for stepping outside the box of traditional team building?

Spark the Flame: Schedule a DiSC facilitator to come in to assess and train your team. DiSC will provide a common language and learning points that help promote appreciation and recognition of the strengths of each team member.

Why

"Great minds have purposes, others have wishes."

—Washington Irving, author

Do you want to have more control over your life? Do you sometimes feel like the economy, or your spouse, business partner, boss or customers, create a reality for you that seems overwhelming? You are not alone.

The "why" is your vision of who you want to be and where you want to go. There should be a company vision, a team mission, and an individual plan to help you implement your goals. The "why" keeps your team real and on target.

Client Story: I do what I do because I love the impact it makes on the companies I work with as well as the individual team members. But I recently found an even greater "why": I created a community service program to combat the violence I've seen in the schools. It teaches parents and teachers a new, innovative way to guide children to focus on their unique gifts so that they're less susceptible to negative influences. My goal is to spread the word through the corporate world and get more companies to sponsor this program in their local schools and community centers. Sponsors get recognition via releases my company sends to the media in the sponsor's name. The community benefits, the company benefits, and I get to use my unique gifts to serve a greater purpose. Win, win, win.

Personal Story: Regret is an emotion I want to avoid. I was greatly impacted by someone who held my hand at the end of his life and said, "I wish..." Have you ever made a choice in your life and later regretted the decision not to act? Have you ever thought back to that lost opportunity and wondered, what if? I do not choose to live my life that way. I want to look back at the end, hold a loved one's hand, and say, "I did. I gave. I bled. I enjoyed. I served. I lived."

As a team leader, you can regard your "why" as the glue of your team vision board. It's what holds everything together. It's what differentiates a team that overcomes challenge and strives for greatness from one that settles into complacency.

"Who you have to be" is more important than "what you have to do" when it comes to achieving your goals. What attributes must you acquire in order to get where you want to go?

Questions to Ponder: Why do you do what you do? Do you wake up excited and ready to face the world? If not, do you want to? Does your company have a vision or mission statement? Do the goals and actions of your team align with that statement? How can you create a strong reason for you and each team member to stay focused and motivated?

Spark the Flame: Right now, pick up a pen and paper and write down the mission of your team. If you can't do it fairly quickly, without looking it up in the manual or on your computer, then it's not resonating with you. If it's not resonating with you as the leader, there's a good chance the team is lost. Sit down and discuss it with the team this week.

X-ray

*"If conversation was the lyrics, laughter was the music,
making time spent together a melody that could be
replayed over and over without getting stale."*

—Nicholas Sparks, novelist

Everyone has some redeeming features; sometimes you just have to look closer to find them. I jest...But seriously, if you want to build stronger, longer-lasting business relationships, you need to go beyond superficial connections and reveal the person within.

In every situation, delving deeper can serve both parties.

If you want to make a sale, it's helpful to do background research on the company, and then during the meeting ask questions to find out more about who they are and what they want. A potential new client will rarely spill all their challenges and goals without some prompting and questions from you.

It doesn't stop at the sale. Once you have the client, continually learning about their business will build a stronger relationship and help you discover other products or services they might require. If you want to grow your business by cross-selling, you need to delve into the full range of your client's needs and stay in contact on a regular basis.

In the world of teams, where the relationships are ongoing and intensive, it's helpful to keenly understand the other members' needs. For better company productivity and flow, learn the requirements and functions of other departments and positions.

The more you learn, the deeper you go, the stronger the relationship.

Client Story: I conducted training for the sales department at a telephone company. We discussed listening, bonding and rapport; needs and wants; emotional buying; and various sales strategies. Then we broke into two groups and put together a sales contest. I was to be available for questions and coaching by phone, and then I'd come back the next month, see who won the contest, and discuss why. The next day the leader of Group A called me to ask why they needed to take so much time and energy for "interrogations of the customers." I explained that interrogation was the opposite of what I was recommending; I said that observing and building a relationship based on genuine interest in the other would ultimately lead to sales. Then I told him my iceberg analogy (below). Group A outsold Group B by 60%.

In addition to the X-ray concept, the iceberg analogy can be helpful.

The iceberg has been used to represent different theories, the most common of which is Freud's description of the tip of the iceberg as the conscious mind and the part below the surface as the subconscious mind.

I use the iceberg to illustrate understanding behavior and building rapport. The top of the iceberg is what people show you easily. You see their company, their role, maybe a picture of a diploma or even one of their kids. Some of it is superficial, the image they want to project via what they are wearing or what their office looks like, or when they talk about the weather to avoid giving away more. In sales, it could be the response, "It's about price." The tip of the iceberg is logic based.

The larger portion of the iceberg, below the surface, is everything that makes them who they are or do what they do--their experiences, education, perspective, mentors, challenges, pain, fear, values, beliefs and concerns. The bottom of the iceberg is emotion based.

When you put on the snorkeling gear and go below the surface (by asking questions and listening), you may discover that "It's about price" is really a cover for "The other vendor brings me donuts each week, I don't like change, frankly I'm not sure I trust you enough to recommend you--and you look a little like the girl who dumped me in 7th grade."

If you spend all your time focusing on lowering your price and trying to compromise based on the erroneous original comment, you miss an opportunity to laugh about the resemblance and coach them through the benefits of change, including better service and continued donuts.

The leader of Group A found the following questions to be very illuminating: "What part of the iceberg caused the Titanic to sink? Isn't it important to discover what's below the surface?"

Questions to Ponder: Is there a specific person you want to get to know better? What is the potential benefit that could stem from learning more? How can the X-ray and iceberg analogies help your team? Anything else you can think of to break through the wall and build a stronger relationship?

Spark the Flame: Create a list of relationship-building questions to distribute to your team. Accept their responses with an open mind. Recommended questions include:

What do you like best about your job?

What would you change to make it more fulfilling?

Do you think you have talents that aren't being used? If so, what are they?

What drives you?

How do you like to be rewarded for a job well done?

Do you have any recommendations on how to make the team more efficient?

Are there any resources you need to help you be more effective in your role?

Other comments?

You

"It is our choices, Harry, that show us what we really are, far more than our abilities."

—Dumbledore to Harry in
Harry Potter and the Chamber of Secrets

It all begins with you.

Many times we define ourselves by our roles--team leader, boss, peer, spouse, parent, friend. Our roles are what we do, not who we are, and we are intrinsically perfect no matter if we are unhappy or less than completely successful in one of our roles. It's important to fully comprehend that our roles do not define us.

But speaking of roles, let's look at the team-leader position for a moment. It generally comprises two areas: managing and leading.

As a manager, you are in charge of the details and organization of objectives and performance. As a leader, you are in charge of the dynamics of human relationships. Both are significant. You might find you're more comfortable in one role than the other. Look to embrace your natural talents while taking steps to improve in the other area to be a winning leader.

Client Story: My business was heavy into executive coaching when my boys were young. It worked because I didn't want to travel as much at that point and I was still serving a need in the marketplace. But one night I realized that many clients' conversations were transitioning from marketing, sales and service to personal issues. There was a distinct pattern of people expressing dissatisfaction with where they were. I was hearing comments like "I don't even like this business" and "It's a family business...there was no other choice." Many wanted more. I decided to research the market to find commonalities, and that's how my first book, *Find Your Fire at Forty*, was born. It told a story, gave suggestions, and provided concrete steps you could take to find your unique gifts and use them to serve others. The point is, if you are searching for more, you're not alone. Know with conviction that the answers lie within you, and you'll find them if you look closely enough.

I believe strongly in the power of the choices we make. You control your thoughts. You control your feelings. You control your actions. You cannot control other people's thoughts, feelings or actions. Accept this, and you can fully comprehend the command you have of your life.

Personal Story: I was once at a crossroads in my life, discontented with where I was but unwilling to make a change. Have you ever been in that place? Just comfortable enough to exist but nowhere near where you think you could be, nowhere near happy. A brush with the fragility of life gave me the impetus to step outside my comfort zone and take action toward opportunity and possibility. I want you to step outside your comfort zone and realize all that is possible for you. To do, have and be every ounce of your potential.

Questions to Ponder: Do you realize and appreciate all that is good about you? Do you know what you want and where you want to go? Is there anything you need to learn or do to be a better leader? What can you do to become more comfortable being uncomfortable?

Spark the Flame: Create a personal mission statement, a balanced one that covers who you want to be in all areas of your life. Print a large version to hang on your bedroom or bathroom mirror and print a small version to laminate and carry in your wallet or purse. The key is to have several ways to keep the mission at the front of your mind as often as possible.

"Be your best, love yourself, live your life with every ounce of you....and your mere presence will inspire everyone you touch."

—Heather Hansen O'Neill

Zig zag

"Intelligence is the handmaiden of flexibility and change."

—Vernor Vinge, computer scientist
and science-fiction author

Creativity, adaptability and flexibility combine to create a foundation for team and relationship potential.

We've established that standard systems, procedures and concrete ways of doing business contribute to your team's success. The next step is to acknowledge the role of flexibility.

The world is filled with new values, new ways of doing business, daily and hourly changes in technology, new work arrangements, and interesting family dynamics. As a leader in a changing world, you have most likely learned to bend and sway with the times. Flexibility is the skill of career longevity. It doesn't mean change for the sake of change, more adaptability to new ideas, technologies and at times management or team personnel.

Minor adjustments can have major ramifications. I'm not a sailor, but I was told that being even slightly off-course can land you in a far different place than you'd planned. If your target is an island, even a minor deviation from your course can leave you lost in open water, with no landmarks by which to correct your course. When you can't see your target, your impulse may be to just keep going, but you'll be going further in the wrong direction and getting farther from your goal. Has this ever happened in your business or life?

Identify team challenges and deal with them before you get too far off course.

Client Story: One of my creative clients was a local fuel company that made a very minor adjustment to its marketing that resulted in a huge response. On each of their monthly invoices, they added a product or service of the month. There was zero cost in doing this other than the time to come up with the monthly promotion. The invoices were being sent anyway. They just made a minor addition that catapulted their per-client profit.

Personal Story: I may be a motivational speaker, but that doesn't mean I don't have doubts and fears. I go through periods of uncertainty just like anyone else. One thing that has helped me immensely is stopping myself before a negative thought immobilizes me. And I change my mind. Simple? Not always. Occasionally there's an internal argument if I'm hungry or particularly crabby. But I insert a more positive thought and fake it until it becomes a new reality. Change your mind, change your reality. We have the power to shift our emotional state based on the thoughts we create and focus on.

But sometimes *change* is forced upon us and we need to come to terms with it before we can use it in the most powerful and productive way.

Change of job status.

Change of relationship status.

Change of demographic.

Change of tax bracket.

Change of life.

Any of these sound familiar?

Change can cause us to become fearful about an unknown future and feel out of control.

Interestingly enough, change is also the impetus for growth, opportunity and unlimited potential. Our ability to learn from, and adapt to, change is what determines our fate and our feeling of having control of our situation.

Questions to Ponder: Are you stuck? What can you do differently to motivate your team? How can you incorporate more innovative strategies? Is change something that comes naturally to you, or does it cause you stress? How can becoming more flexible make you a more effective team leader?

Spark the Flame: Think of a problem you are currently experiencing and brainstorm a full page of solutions. Don't hold back. Do not judge the ideas that come to mind; simply add them to the list. Sometimes the most obscure thought can lead to the most productive one. You might find an answer that's more inventive than you'd anticipated. If you find value in this exercise, use it at your next team meeting and see how the creative solutions multiply.

Special Bonus Resources:

For reinforcement, support and added value, I've created an exclusive link for book buyers only. It will include:

- ✓ Resources
- ✓ An inspirational audio program
- ✓ Special access to a monthly team building Q&A
- ✓ And more!

Go to www.fireinfive.com/bookresources and enter your name and email address to receive your *Teams On Fire!* **bonus page.**

To request information about corporate keynotes, workshops, or our community connection program:

Call 203-312-4990 or email Heather at heather@ fireinfive.com

Mention *Teams On Fire!* and you will receive a complimentary discovery session valued at $500.

Call 203-312-4990 today
or
visit www.fireinfive.com